P9-CML-303

WEST GA REG LIB SYS
Neva Lomason
Memorial Library

The World of Work

Choosing a Career in Cosmetology

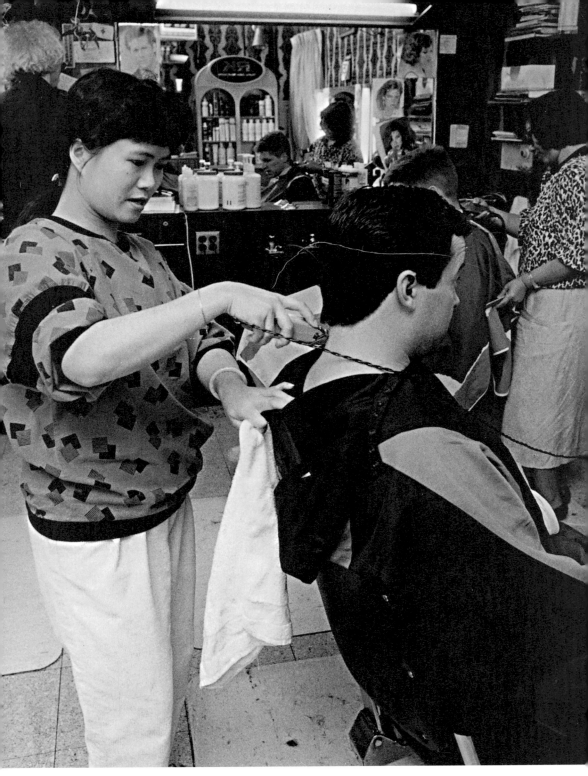

Cosmetology is an exciting field that offers more opportunities every year.

The World of Work

Choosing a Career in Cosmetology

Jeanne M. Strazzabosco

THE ROSEN PUBLISHING GROUP, INC.
NEW YORK

Published in 1997 by The Rosen Publishing Group, Inc.
29 East 21st Street, New York, NY 10010

Copyright © 1997 by The Rosen Publishing Group, Inc.

All rights reserved. No part of this book may be reproduced in any form without permission in writing from the publisher, except by a reviewer.

First Edition

Manufactured in the United States of America

Library of Congress Cataloging–in–Publication Data
Strazzabosco, Jeanne.
    Choosing a career in cosmetology: Jeanne M. Strazzabosco.—1st ed.
        p.   cm.—(The world of work)
    Summary: Discusses a variety of careers in cosmetology, the
necessary education, potential salaries, and benefits.
    Includes bibliographical references and index.
    ISBN 0-8239-2279-0
    1. Beauty culture—Vocational guidance—Juvenile literature.
[1. Beauty culture—Vocational guidance.   2. Vocational guidance.]
I. Title.   II. Series: World of work (New York, N.Y.)
TT958.S77   1996
646.7′2′023—dc20
                                                                    96-16968
                                                                       CIP
                                                                        AC

Contents

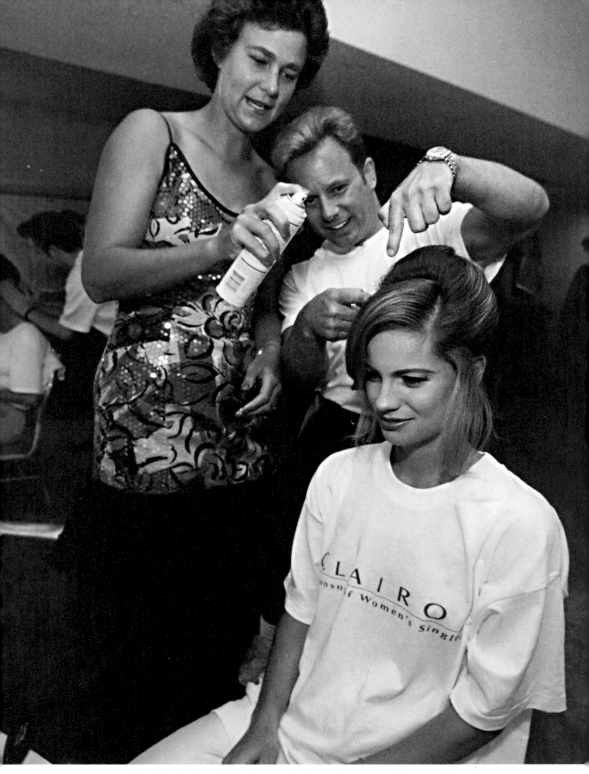

Working in the field of cosmetology allows you to be creative.

The World of Cosmetology

1

Welcome to the world of cosmetology! Cosmetology is an exciting field with many opportunities. The training period is fairly short for careers in this field. You can also earn a lot of money. And right now there is a great need for people in the beauty industry. The number of salons and jobs has risen two percent every year since 1986. About 15,000 positions open up every year.

This look inside the field of cosmetology will help you make some decisions about your future. It will help you look at your skills and interests to find out if this is the right career choice for you. You will read about the many different careers that cosmetology offers, as well as how to pursue them.

The field of cosmetology has many areas. It includes salon owners, hairdressers, beauty school directors and teachers, estheticians, nail and skin experts, image consultants, and salon receptionists. Some people in these careers are college graduates. Others have high school diplomas. There are also men and women who had been successful in other professions but were unhappy with their jobs. They changed to cosmetology to be successful, satisfied, and happy in their careers.

Most people in cosmetology are very excited about their careers. They like what they do. They are confident and take pride in their jobs. One hairdresser says, "The best part of what I do is that I can really help people. I can change how a person looks at himself and how the world looks at that person in a short period of time." Cosmetology is one of the few careers in which you can see the results of your work immediately. When a hairdresser, nail technician, or image consultant finishes with a client, he or she immediately gets feedback. That feedback is often positive, which makes you feel very good about what you do.

Here are some of the exciting careers that await you in the wide field of cosmetology:

- Manicurist
- Hairdresser
- Wig Technician
- Image Consultant

- Color Specialist
- Natural Hairdresser
- Skin Care Specialist/Esthetician
- Retail Specialist in Beauty Products
- Specialist in Aromatherapy and Massage
- Instructor
- Beauty Salon Manager
- Cosmetic Artist
- Salon Owner
- Permanent Wave Technician
- Nail Technician
- Salon Operator
- Freelance Cosmetologist

Questions to Ask Yourself

Cosmetology is a popular field. It offers many job opportunities. 1) How can you find out about jobs in your area? 2) What are some of the careers that are available in cosmetology?

Is Cosmetology the Right Career for Me? 2

You may not be sure whether or not you want to go to college. You may be looking for a way to pay for your college education. You might feel like one young hairdresser who tried several careers. He was successful in all of them, but none felt like the right match. He was neither happy nor satisfied with how he was earning a living. He just didn't know what he wanted to do with his life. But then he tried cosmetology. It felt like the right fit.

It's never too early or too late to explore career options. Gather as much information as possible before making a decision as important as how you're going to earn a living. You've already made a good start by reading this book.

Getting Started

You may be wondering if you have the necessary traits to pursue a career in cosmetology. After all, you're about to invest a fair

There are a variety of careers you can choose from. These range from hairdresser to skin care specialist.

amount of time and money in training. Ask yourself some questions that will help you find out whether you have the qualities that it takes to succeed.

• *Do you like to be around people? Are you comfortable talking to people you may not know?*

Salon owners, beauty school directors, hairdressers, nail technicians, and other cosmetologists all stress the importance of having good social skills. You have to be able to make clients feel comfortable. It's equally important to be able to communicate with

11

coworkers in order to keep a pleasant and professional work atmosphere.

• *Are you outgoing? Do you consider yourself a warm and friendly person?*

Successful *cosmetologists*, people in the field of cosmetology, want to please their clients. Your success is tied to your ability to keep your customers coming back. If you have talent, an outgoing personality, and a genuine interest in people, you have a great opportunity to build a loyal following of clients.

• *Are you willing to deal with "the public?"*

Cosmetologists provide a service for their clients. Your job is to help your clients look as good as they possibly can. However, not all of your clients will be easy to get along with. You'll need to perfect and rely on your "people skills." These skills help you serve all kinds of people.

• *Do you have a high energy level? Are you in good health?*

As a hairdresser you may find yourself working long and irregular hours. Some days you may have appointments at 8:00 a.m. Other days you may work until 9:00 p.m. You will probably spend most of your day on your feet. Your ability to produce high-quality work quickly affects the amount of money you can earn. The more clients you can see in a day, the more money you can earn.

• *Do you have an artistic eye? Do you like trying out new hairstyles or different ways of wearing cosmetics? Do you follow fashion trends?*

Just like fashion, the world of cosmetology changes with every season. Being able to adapt to change or to create new styles will help you become successful. You must also be artistic. As a cosmetologist you'll help people make decisions about how they look, whether it's hairstyle, hair color and texture, nails, or how they wear their makeup. You want them to be confident in your ability to guide them through decisions about their image.

To be successful and happy with your career, you must like what you're doing. A successful cosmetologist must like people, be energetic, enjoy providing a service, and have an interest in fashion. If you answered yes to most of the questions above, a career in cosmetology may be a good choice for you.

Questions to Ask Yourself

There are several things to consider when you

decide whether a career in cosmetology is for you. 1) Do you have the traits and skills that are necessary to be successful in the field of cosmetology? 2) If so, which skills do you have? 3) If not, how can you get these skills?

Career Possibilities

3

As you read in Chapter 1, there are many different careers within the field of cosmetology. Here are a few descriptions to give you an idea of the variety of careers.

Salon Receptionist

The *receptionist* in a salon is the first person a client sees and talks to. It is essential that all clients be greeted warmly and pleasantly and, if possible, called by name.

A receptionist has many tasks. As a receptionist, you'll find your day very busy. In addition to greeting the clients, you'll answer the phone, record appointments, and let the hairdressers know that their clients have arrived. You'll also recommend to clients other services and products that the salon offers. You'll need to know about the products in order to help clients. You may be asked to help restock the shelves or clean up.

Each state in the United States requires

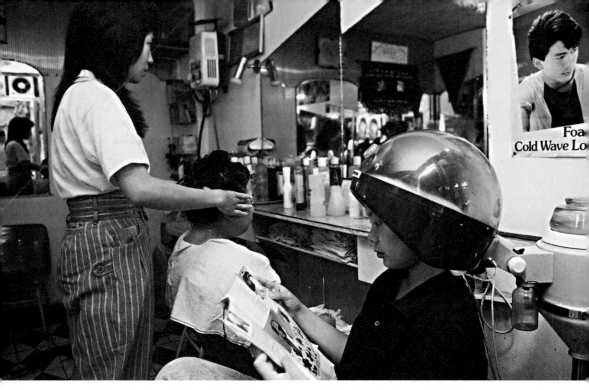

Whether in a high-profile salon or in a neighborhood salon, a hairdresser must know the current trends in hairstyles.

cosmetologists to have special licenses to practice. A receptionist in a salon doesn't need a *cosmetology license*. However, some cosmetologists start out as receptionists and decide to go to cosmetology school to get their cosmetology licenses once they see what a career in the field is like.

Sabrina, Hairdresser

"Sabrina, your 3:00 appointment is here. She's in the waiting room," said Randy. "Tonight is Brenda's prom. She looks nervous."

Sabrina had just finished her last customer. She had no time to relax, but she said cheer-

fully, "Thanks, Randy. I'm ready for her."

Sabrina greeted Brenda warmly before leading her to her chair. Sabrina chats with her clients before she starts the shampoo. She finds it a good way to put them at ease and find out exactly what they want done to their hair.

"So tonight is the big night. How do you want to wear your hair, Brenda?" Sabrina asked.

"Oh, I haven't got a clue. You're going to have to help me."

Sabrina asked Brenda what her dress was like. Then she showed Brenda some photographs of different styles that might complement her dress as well as the shape of her face. They settled on a style, and Sabrina brought Brenda to the shampoo area.

A half-hour later Brenda looked into the mirror and was thrilled with what she saw. "Sabrina, you are the best. I can't believe how great my hair looks." The other hairdressers admired Sabrina's work as they walked by her station. Sabrina felt proud as she put the finishing touches on Brenda's hair.

Your day as a *hairdresser* is filled with great moments of personal pride. If you are good and keep up with current trends, you will probably receive positive feedback every day if not several times a day. It is an incredible feeling to make a person feel good about the way he or she looks.

First you have to decide where you'd like to work. Would you prefer a small neighborhood salon or a large national chain? A chain is a *franchise*, or many salons that have the same name and are run in the same style, such as Jean Louis David or The Lemon Tree. Perhaps you'd enjoy working in a department store salon. You have to decide what's best for you. You may start out in a large salon and then decide to move to a small salon. As you research potential jobs, ask questions that will help you make a good decision. These include questions like the following:

- What will your hours be like?
- How much can you expect to earn?
- Are there benefits such as health or life insurance?
- What is the vacation policy?
- Is there opportunity for advancement?

A hairdresser's day is fast-paced and full. You have many responsibilities. Your work station must always be clean. It must be equipped with all the products that you will

As a hairdresser, you help people make important decisions about how they will look.

need for the day. You'll check with the receptionist to see who your clients are and what services they want that day. You will want to know if you are going to do any permanents or hair color treatments so that you'll have all the curlers and supplies handy. You have to watch the time carefully. You don't want to keep clients waiting. Some hairdressers keep a record of their customers' hair colors or tints. That way it's easier to mix the color quickly and accurately for the customer every time. Some salons keep records of their clients' treatments in their computer systems.

Now you're ready to greet your clients. The receptionist will let you know when they arrive. However, it is your job to keep an eye on the time so that you're always ready for them. In most salons you will be responsible for doing your customers' shampoos as well as the cut, style, or other hair treatment.

You may provide any of the following services to your client:

- haircut
- set and style
- scalp massage
- hair color and toning
- corrective hair color

- wig and hairpiece care and style
- permanent waves
- beard trim
- scalp treatments for dryness and dandruff
- highlighting hair
- hair straightening
- scalp treatments for thinning hair

Sometimes clients are nervous about having their hair done. You must help them relax and feel more at ease. A hairdresser must be personable and friendly, and feel comfortable talking with people.

You may have a couple of short breaks as well as a lunch or dinner break in your day. But aside from these breaks you will be busy every minute. If you're not with a client, you may be folding towels, stocking beauty products, sweeping and cleaning your work station, or helping out the receptionist if the salon is busy.

Keep in mind that you are in the business of making people look good. You are your own best advertisement. You want to convince your clients that you can help them look good. In order to do that, *you* need to look good. Your own hair should be cut and styled to reflect current trends. You should be well groomed and properly dressed. If your salon sells certain lines of beauty products, learn how they are used. As a hairdresser you are a walking advertisement for the services and the products sold in the salon.

You must conduct yourself professionally. Your customers probably don't want to hear about your personal life. The salon's professional reputation as well as your ability to establish and maintain loyal customers depend on your ability to act professionally. Keep a positive attitude and don't bring your personal problems into the workplace.

Your success as a hairdresser also rests on your ability to continue learning and growing. It is very important to keep up on current trends in hairdressing. You may attend hair shows to learn new techniques for hair treatment. Some salons will even pay for you to go to *trade shows*. Trade shows are usually held in hotels or convention centers. Professional hairdressers from all over a region or state gather to learn and share techniques, products, and new styles. Reading beauty and hair magazines will help you keep up on changes in the beauty business.

Finally, remember that you're in this business because you want to help people feel

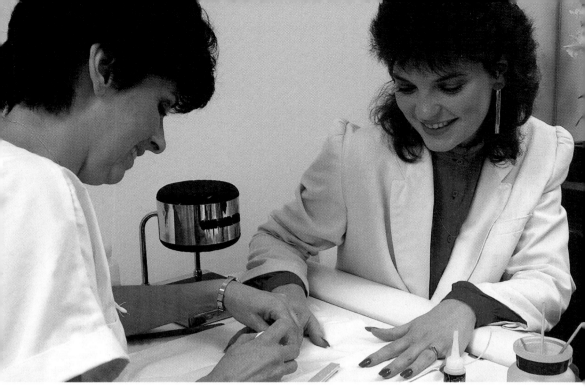

More and more people are getting manicures regularly. The demand for nail technicians is growing.

good about the way they look. You supply a very important service.

Kara, Nail Technician

Kara has just arrived in the salon. She checks to see how many clients she has tonight. Kara works evenings and weekends as a nail technician. During the day she goes to a community college. Her schedule doesn't leave her much room for a social life, but she figures it's worth it. Her job as nail technician is paying for college. She completed her training during her senior year of high school at a career center.

"Hey, Kara. You've got a busy night ahead

of you—five manicures, one pedicure, and three sets of acrylic nails. Don't worry, only one of them needs appliqués, too," says Paulina.

"Thanks, Paulina. How long before my first client arrives?"

"You've got about 15 minutes."

"Perfect, just enough time to check my polishes and set up," says Kara. "Got to run! See you on my break!"

Once Kara reaches her station she feels at home. She loves setting up her manicure supplies and getting the cleansing solutions and lotions ready. She checks the polishes to make sure all the available colors are displayed. The nails she creates are really works of art, so to Kara, her nail station is more like a studio.

In comes her first client, Isabelle. "Kara, what a day I've had."

"How are you doing, Isabelle? It's good to see you. Tell me all about it," says Kara.

Kara is genuinely interested in Isabelle's life. Kara listens as Isabelle tells of the day's adventures. All the while Kara works on Isabelle's manicure. Kara knows that this manicure is one of the small pleasures Isabelle allows herself. She puts all her energy and talent into making Isabelle's nails look great. As always, Isabelle is pleased with Kara's efforts.

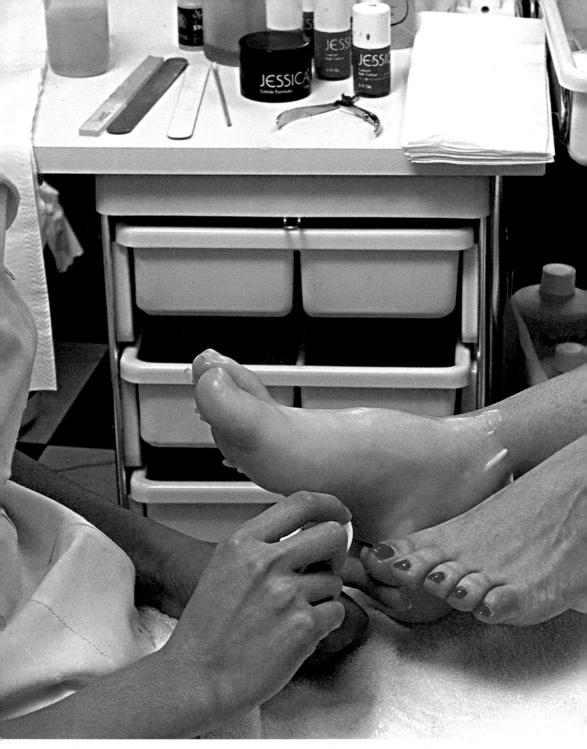

Services such as manicures and pedicures are deeply appreciated and enjoyed by clients. A nail technician can often take pride in having made clients happy and relaxed.

Kara's next client steps in and the evening rolls by. Kara works on her clients' hands attentively all night. She smiles and listens to their stories. She fills in this one's acrylic nails and hand-paints moons and stars on that one's nails. She gently massages a woman's feet before giving her a pedicure. At the end of the night, she cleans up her station and checks out for the night. Once home, she grabs a glass of juice and begins to study for the psychology test she has the next morning.

Manicures, the professional care of one's hands and fingernails, used to be considered a luxury. Today they are a service that many people enjoy. Men and woman regularly use the services of professional *nail technicians*.

The rising popularity of acrylic, or fake, nails has also increased business for nail technicians.

As a nail technician, your specialty is the care and treatment of fingernails and toenails. You should have a good understanding of the structure of hands, arms, feet, and nails. Knowing the cosmetics used in manicuring is essential. So is the ability to give high-quality manicures and pedicures efficiently.

You must also regularly disinfect and sanitize your instruments and work station.

Massage is another part of this career. One of the nicest parts of a manicure or a pedicure is the massage. A manicure may include a hand and arm massage. A pedicure, the professional care of one's feet and toenails, may include a foot and leg massage. Some nail technicians practice a new technique called *reflexology*. Reflexology is the deep massage of specific points in the hands and feet.

Just like a hairdresser, a nail technician is in the business of helping a client feel good about the way he or she looks. A nail technician provides a service that is important and appreciated. At the end of the day you can be proud that you've helped people feel good about themselves.

You will have to decide whether you want to work in a nails-only salon or in a full-service salon. If you choose a full-service salon, you will probably be the only nail technician there. That means that you will have all the nail clients. However, you won't have other nail technicians to consult with. And there may be no one to fill in for you when you're sick or on vacation.

As an esthetician you may choose from a variety of career options, from giving facials to selling cosmetics.

As a nail technician, you may provide any of these services to your clients:

- manicures
- acrylic, or fake, nails
- paraffin, or wax, treatments for nails
- foot, leg massage
- nail mending
- pedicures
- hand, arm massage
- nail wrapping to strengthen nails

Nikki, Esthetician/Skin Care Specialist

Nikki had been working in Helen's salon for

three years as a hairdresser. She enjoyed what she was doing. Nikki had a natural radiance. Her skin seemed to glow. Ever since she was a teen she had eaten a healthy diet and taken care of her skin. She was always trying out new skin treatments.

Nikki's clients often asked her what her secret was. They complimented her on her healthy complexion. One day Nikki approached Helen, the owner of the salon, with the idea that the salon could offer skin care and that she'd like to be involved.

The salon had top-notch hairdressers and a very successful following. After talking with Nikki, Helen decided to look into the idea of offering skin care to their clients. After all, they were in the business of making people look good, and that didn't end with hair.

Helen sent Nikki to seminars sponsored by skin care specialists and beauty product companies. Together they created a skin care program with a full line of services for their clients. The program had a great response and was soon in high demand.

As a *skin care specialist*, or *esthetician*, you have many choices. You could work in a salon or teach. You could travel giving demonstrations at beauty shows. Or you could become a consultant for a cosmetics company. You could work for one cosmetics company or freelance for several. You could even create new products.

As an esthetician, you work to help your clients look and feel good. You need to know about different skin types so that you can advise your clients about what skin care products to use. You should be an expert about the products you offer and use. It's essential to read everything available about the products. You should go to seminars run by beauty product manufacturers.

You must understand the structure of skin and be able to identify skin disorders. You should be able to tell apart skin disorders that you can treat from those that need to be seen by a doctor.

You may offer facial and neck massages. In order to be effective, you must know all the structures involved, including muscles, nerves, and blood vessels.

As an esthetician you may offer a wide variety of services, from facials to cosmetics application. You will help your clients look and feel as terrific as they can. Some estheticians offer color consultation. That

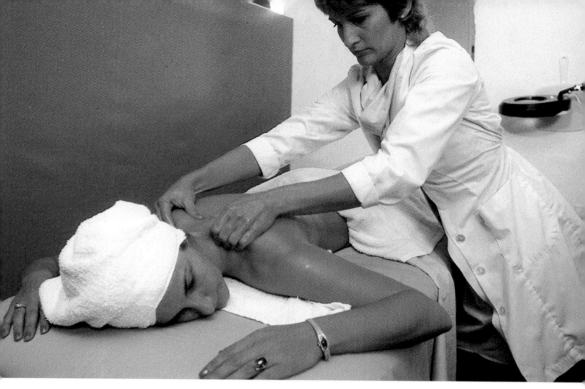

One popular service that some salons offer are massages. These can range from facial massages to full-body massages.

means they help clients find the colors of clothing, makeup, and hair that best suit their own natural coloring.

You may even get into *image consulting*. Clients will come to you to find out how they should dress or style their hair or generally conduct themselves for their professions.

As an esthetician, you may offer any of the following services to your clients:

- massage
- exfoliation — cleaning the pores in the skin on a person's face
- masks

- color consultation
- facial/skin cleansing
- waxing/hair removal
- makeup application and instruction
- skin care analysis

Michael, Salon Owner

Michael had worked in more than a dozen salons. He was a terrific hairdresser. He established a huge following in each of these salons. At the last salon in which he worked he had approached his boss, Anthony, about becoming part owner of the salon. Michael had made many good suggestions over the last two years that had made a positive difference in the salon.

Anthony appreciated Michael's interest, but he didn't think he could afford a partner. Michael was disappointed, but he wasn't discouraged. He checked his savings account and talked to various lending agencies. Then he decided to open his own shop.

Michael started out with two employees besides himself and his wife, Kim. Twelve years later he has more than 30 employees and is thinking of moving his salon to a larger building. His salon offers a wide range of hair, nail, and skin services. His clients love to come to his salon because the staff is knowledgeable, talented, professional, and friendly.

In addition to running the salon, Michael still does hair. He says he'll never give it up because he loves it. He and his wife do free-lance work too. Kim is an image consultant and works with many large corporations. They both believe in giving back to the people who provide them with their cosmetologists. They frequently lecture and do demonstrations at area career centers and cosmetology schools.

Owning and operating your own salon can be a thrilling career. As *owner* you have many responsibilities. You are responsible for personnel. You'll have to decide what services you'll offer so that you can hire the right staff. You'll interview, hire, and manage the training of all staff members. At various points during the year, you will meet with each of your employees in order to evaluate his or her performance.

A successful salon has rules for the employees to follow. These rules may include how employees should dress, how they should behave while in the salon, whether personal calls will be allowed at work, and what to do when someone is late for work or calls in sick. These are essential for the day-to-day operation to run smoothly. You need to set these rules and make sure they are followed.

As owner you are responsible for the financial management of the business. As you pay your employees, you'll keep track of the profits. You'll decide which beauty products are used and sold. You'll manage the purchase of all the necessary products and equipment.

It may sound overwhelming, but with good planning, good management skills, and a talented support staff you can create an enjoyable and profitable career for yourself as a salon owner.

Cosmetology Instructor

There are careers in cosmetology outside the salon. A licensed cosmetologist can work as an *instructor* in a *career center* or *cosmetology school*. This can be an equally rewarding and profitable career. As an instructor, you will help people learn the skills necessary to begin their careers in cosmetology. You may find the regular hours appealing.

Most states require instructors to have additional training and a certain amount of salon experience. A genuine interest in young people is essential if you seek this career. Advising and counseling will also be part of your role as instructor.

These are just some of the jobs in the world of cosmetology. You might talk to your local hairdresser, nail technician, or salon owner for more insights into these or other careers.

Earning Potential

Although the national average salary for a cosmetologist is approximately $18,000 to $20,000 a year, salaries differ greatly among salons and among professions. In one salon in a suburb of Rochester, New York, hairdressers in their early twenties make between $35,000 and $40,000 a year.

Many cosmetologists earn a salary plus a percentage of the "sales," or the money that their clients paid for their services. This is called a *commission*. In some salons cosmetologists also receive a commission on the beauty products they sell to their clients. It is difficult to estimate total earnings because most cosmetologists receive tips in addition to salaries and commissions. In larger salons, department stores, and hotels, cosmetologists may be offered *benefits* such as health insurance.

The Hours You Work

Full-time cosmetologists work 40 hours or more a week. That usually includes some evening and weekend hours. Evenings and weekends are the busy times for beauty salons. Even *part-time* employees may find themselves working evenings and weekends.

Freelance Work

Some cosmetologists choose to earn their living doing *freelance* work. They don't work for one particular salon; they work for themselves and set their own hours. A freelance cosmetologist may be hired to style the hair of an entire bridal party so that the party doesn't have to go to a salon. He or she might do an actor's makeup for a local commercial. One freelance hairdresser said that he was responsible for styling the hair of the players and their wives for the Ryder Cup golf tournament.

Questions to Ask Yourself

There are a wide variety of careers in cosmetology. 1) Which field do you find most appealing? 2) What do you like most about that field? 3) What do you like least?

Training

In order to pursue a career in cosmetology you must successfully complete a *training program*. The fact that you have been cutting and styling your brother's or sister's hair since you were 14 does not mean you can take your talents out to the public yet. You must first be properly trained. Once you have successfully completed your training program, you can take your state's licensing examination for cosmetology. Every state in the United States requires that you pass its licensing test before you can work as a cosmetologist.

Career Centers

If you are still in high school, you have a couple of ways to get training. Many states have *vocational* or *trade schools* that work with public high schools. Vocational schools are really career centers that offer courses in cosmetology as well as other areas, such as auto services, business, computer technology,

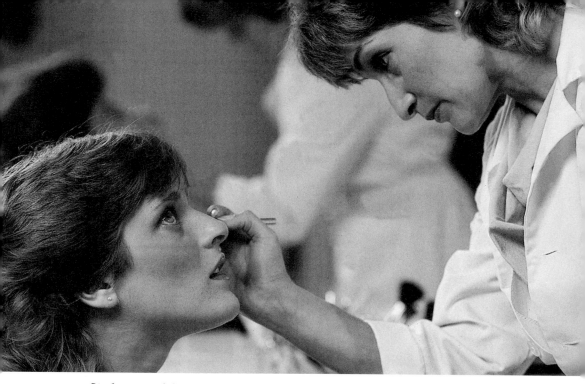

Students studying cosmetology can learn everything from applying makeup to hair dressing to giving manicures at a vocational school.

metal trades, and child care. Most programs are designed for 10th to 12th graders. The goal is to provide an environment in which students can develop the necessary skills for a particular career. They offer practical experience. Many career centers even provide on-the-job experiences in the community.

The programs offer you the opportunity to attend classes at your high school for half of the day. You attend classes at the vocational center for the other half of the day. This schedule works well for many students. They can complete their requirements for a high school diploma and train for a career at the same time. Then they are able to earn high school credits that work toward a high school diploma. These credits replace some of the required courses they would ordinarily take at high school. It's important to do well in both career center and high school classes because in today's competitive market, a high school diploma is a must.

Getting Started at a Career Center

First you need to find out if there are any career centers in your area. The best place to do this is in your own high school career counseling center. Ask one of your counselors if there is a career center or vocational school that offers cosmetology in your area. Ask your counselor if anyone from your school is enrolled in the program. It is a good idea to talk to someone who is already attending the center to see what they think of it. You may even want to set up a visit so that you can actually see what the school is like and how the classes are run.

Cosmetology departments generally look like huge beauty salons. Each student has his or her own station, which is set up as if it were in a salon. There is a swivel chair, a mirror,

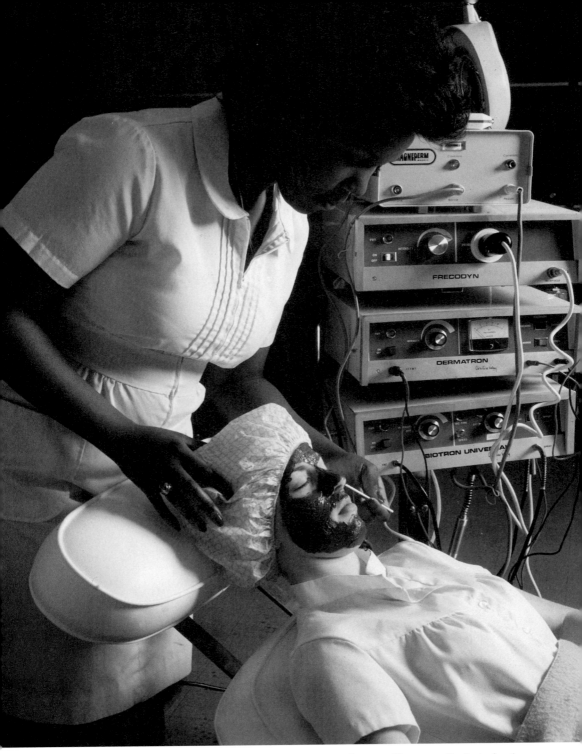

Cosmetology classes consist of classroom study as well as practical study. As a student, you will listen to lectures and practice what you learn on people.

and all the accessories needed to cut and style hair. There are also stations where students practice nail and skin care. Professional beauty products are used for the hands-on practice the students receive. Each student is supplied with a mannequin which is used to practice cutting, styling, and coloring hair.

Cosmetology students also cut and style hair for people as part of their practice. Many centers offer free or reduced-price haircuts and other hair and nail services to senior citizens. Some centers open their schools one day a week to anyone in the community who would like a free haircut or style. This is a great way to involve students in community service while giving them the opportunity to practice the skills they are learning.

Cosmetology Class

Cosmetology classes are broken up into classroom study, lectures, demonstrations, and practice. There are many important things you need to learn before you can pick up a pair of scissors and start cutting hair. You'll learn step-by-step procedures for all the services offered in hair, nail, and skin care. For example, you'll learn about cleaning solutions for combs and scissors. Students learn the relationship between bacteria and the spread of disease so that they can practice safely. While you practice the procedures, you will be watched and guided by your teachers.

Some of the topics covered in cosmetology classes include the following:

- sterilization and sanitation of work stations and tools
- skin care/cosmetics
- hairstyling
- color rinses
- shampoos
- temporary hair removal
- permanent waving
- sculptured nails
- design haircutting and styling
- state board preparation
- advanced hairstyling
- chemical hair straightening
- tinting and bleaching of hair
- scalp and hair treatments
- hair extension and wigs
- salon management and ownership

There are shorter programs for nail and skin care. Topics covered in nail care include sculptured nails, manicures and pedicures, and nail art. In the area of skin care, you would study skin care, makeup application, facial treatments, cosmetic chemistry, nutrition, and waxing.

Length of Programs

Most cosmetology programs offered through career centers run for two and a half years. You start when you are in 11th grade and complete the training by the end of 12th grade. This means that you attend cosmetology classes during the summer between your junior and senior years. Some students begin the program in 10th grade and don't attend classes during the summer.

Cost of the Programs

High schools often cover the cost for student tuition and busing. Some courses may require uniforms or additional safety equipment that you may have to pay for. If any of these costs are going to be difficult or impossible for you, speak to a counselor. Financial assistance is often available.

Advantages of a Career Center

The most important advantage is that you will develop the skills and attitudes necessary to help you find a successful career. One cosmetology instructor said of the career center, "This is not a classroom. This is cosmetology practicing."

In the cosmetology department you will have teachers who are certified in cosmetology. Many of them have salon experience too. You will meet students from different high schools and different backgrounds.

You have all kinds of support staff in addition to your teachers. There are social workers and counselors at the centers to help you. Some centers also offer day-care services. Single parents can bring their children to the center's facility while they attend classes. Financial aid may be available to cover the fees for the day care, which can be discussed with a counselor there.

Career centers sometimes offer field trips and speakers from the field of cosmetology. These help you get a look at career opportunities as well as meet potential employers. Some centers offer placement services, which means that they actually help you find a job.

You not only learn the necessary skills of hair, nail, and skin care, but you learn how to write a good *résumé*. You are prepared for

Vidal Sassoon is an example of a successful member of the field of cosmetology.

interviews. You practice being interviewed. You are counseled on how to dress and how to behave during an interview. Many centers set up a job shadowing placement for you. Job shadowing means that you spend time in a beauty salon observing one or more people who work there. You can also learn useful tips on how to achieve success once you've been placed in a position.

Many students speak of the confidence they feel as they near the end of their training. The many hours of practice they spend pay off in the end. They believe that they have accomplished something useful and practical.

One final advantage that is that your high school often pays the tuition for these centers.

Cosmetology Schools

The other path someone interested in cosmetology can take is to enroll in a *cosmetology school*. You can locate a cosmetology school in your area by looking in the yellow pages of the phone book under beauty or cosmetology schools.

Just as in career centers, cosmetology schools offer the opportunity to learn and practice the necessary skills to be a good cosmetologist. Instructors provide students with comprehensive training that will qualify them to pass a state cosmetology test so that they can obtain a cosmetologist license.

The areas of instruction in a cosmetology school are the same as the programs offered at career centers and are divided between *theory*, or the facts about the subject, and *practice*, or how you put the facts into action. For example, in New York state, there are 15 hours of theory and 15 hours of practice for hair analysis. The number of hours required varies from state to state.

Cosmetology students learn through

demonstration, lecture, discussion, visual aids, classroom practice, and clinical practice. Students are evaluated through tests and quizzes as well as by their classwork. Attendance is crucial. All students must regularly attend classes and demonstrate satisfactory academic progress. Students who do not fulfill these requirements may be put on probation or even expelled from training.

Cosmetology training can last from six months to a year, or longer if you decide to take advanced courses. It all depends on whether you are a full- or part-time student. Many cosmetology schools require that their students have a high school diploma or pass the General Educational Development or GED tests. However, an applicant who does not have a high school diploma or a GED certificate may still be eligible if he or she has a minimum of an eighth grade education and scores well on a written exam provided by the school.

Choosing a Cosmetology School

It's important to do some research before you hand over your hard-earned money for tuition, which high schools don't cover. Schedule an interview with the director of the school you're interested in. Spend a morning at the school seeing how it operates. Cosmetology schools will often give you a list of their faculty. Check to make sure the instructors are licensed cosmetologists. You want to be certain that you will be trained in a professional and safe environment. Talk to some of the students about what they like and dislike about the school.

Ask the director what percentage of the school's graduates pass the licensing examination and find jobs. That will give you an idea of how good the instruction is. Find out if the school helps prepare you for interviews. Many beauty schools set up interviews for their students with potential employers in their area. A beauty salon looking to hire a new hairdresser or nail or skin technician often calls local beauty school or training center to see if they have any qualified candidates.

The Cost

During your interview with the director find out what the cost will be. Make sure there are no hidden fees. Sometimes there are fees for equipment or uniforms that are in addition to the tuition. You don't want to be surprised with extra fees later on.

Cosmetology schools usually cost between $2,000 and $7,000. But don't be scared off by the cost. Most schools let their students pay their tuition over a period of time. *Scholarships* and *financial aid plans* are available as well. The cosmetology school should be able to help you find out if you qualify for financial aid and how to apply for a scholarship. Many independent foundations offer scholarships to candidates who are interested in pursuing a career in cosmetology but can't afford to. Federal and state aid programs are available too. The federal programs help qualified students with tuition costs. In some cases they provide money for meals, transportation, and baby-sitting. Applications for these grants and loans are available at your school, local libraries, and high school counseling centers.

Enrolling in Cosmetology School

Contact the school of your choice to set up an interview with the director or an instructor. At the interview you may be given a tour of the school. You may also receive information about school policies and procedures. Applicants can usually enroll in beauty school any time of the year. There are day and evening classes to help you work training in around your schedule.

You may file an *application* for admission at this point. There is often a registration fee of $50 to $200 with the application. This fee may be nonrefundable. That means that even if you decide *not* to attend the school, the registration fee will not be returned to you. When enrolling, you will need to have some form of identification that proves your age, such as a driver's license, birth certificate, or passport.

Questions to Ask Yourself

Many of the careers in cosmetology require specific training. 1) Where can you get the kind of training that you will need to pursue your career? 2) How can you find out about the programs in your area?

The Cosmetologist
Licensing Examination 5

Once you've completed your training, you must take and pass a *cosmetology licensing examination* for your state. Every state requires cosmetologists to be licensed to practice. There are different licenses within the field. They include hairdressing, skin technician, and nail technician. In fact, some states are now considering a new type of cosmetology license called a *natural hairdressing license*. This is a license that allows you to cut and style hair without using any chemicals in treating hair.

Each state has a required number of hours of practice that must be completed before you can take the licensing test. The hours vary from state to state. For example, if you want to take the Kansas or New York licensing exam for hairdressing, you need 1,000 hours of practice. In Florida, you need 1,200 hours. The number of required hours also differs from profession to profession. The number of

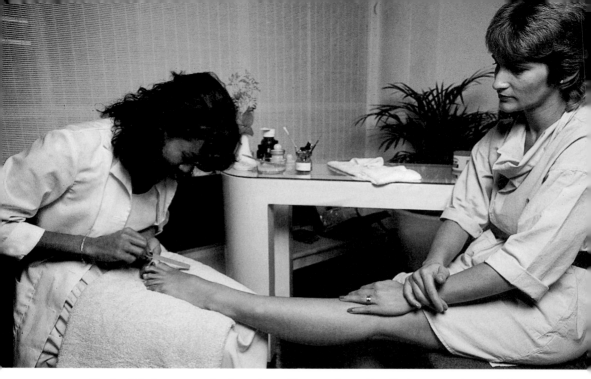

Each state has a required number of hours of practice that you must complete before you can take the cosmetology licensing exam. The required number of hours is less for a nail technician than for a hairdresser.

practice hours required in New York state before you can take the exam for nail technician is 250. The skin care technician license exam requires 500 hours. Your career center or cosmetology school will know the exact number of hours required for your state and your profession. Their program is designed to make sure each student is given the opportunity to practice the required number of hours.

There are two parts to the test—written

and practical. The written part covers factual knowledge, technical information, understanding of principles, and problem-solving abilities related to cosmetology. In the practical part you show the skills that you've learned on live models. You will cut, set, and style the hair of models with different textures of hair. If you are taking a nail technician exam, you will show the various skills that relate to treatment of nails, such as manicure and polish application.

Licensing review books offer practice test questions. There are also review questions in cosmetology textbooks. Study with a friend or a group of friends. Remember that your training was designed to prepare you for the licensing test. Have confidence in the new skills that all your hard work and long hours of practice have brought you.

Questions to Ask Yourself

Every cosmetologist must take and pass the cosmetology licensing exam for his or her state. 1) How can you find out about the requirements for the licensing exam in your state? 2) How can you prepare yourself for taking the exam?

Getting a Job

6

Now that you've completed your training and have passed your state licensing examination, you're ready to find a job. One way to go about entering the field of cosmetology is to begin as an apprentice.

Apprenticing

Apprenticeship is an old practice that is gaining popularity again. In an apprenticeship, you work directly under a *mentor*, an expert in your field. Working as an apprentice gives you a chance to sharpen your existing skills while learning other methods and tips from established professionals. Once you pass (or are close to passing) your licensing examination, you are eligible to apprentice in a salon. You receive a salary, and it is a great opportunity to learn from people who have been in the field for years.

When you begin an apprenticeship, you will work with a particular hairdresser (or other

Professional hairdressers work in a variety of environments. Some hairdressers even go to people's homes.

cosmetologist, depending on the field you've chosen to work in) who has agreed to act as your mentor. At first you'll watch for all kinds of details, not just how your mentor styles or cuts hair. You'll listen to how he or she greets the clients, handles the instruments, and describes various beauty products and services the salon offers. Another very important element you'll see is how your mentor manages time.

Soon you will begin greeting your mentor's clients and getting them ready. This might include doing their shampoos or removing old nail polish. Once your mentor is finished, you'll help the clients check out, make another appointment, or see if they want to buy any beauty products.

Once you feel comfortable, and your mentor is confident in your abilities, you'll begin to see clients of your own. You'll probably feel nervous at first. Just about everyone does. But before long you'll feel comfortable with what you're doing, and the confidence you had during training will return.

Check with the director of your career center or cosmetology school about apprenticeships. He or she should be able to

Many cosmetology schools help their students prepare for interviews. One way to prepare is by doing a pretend interview with a teacher or collegue.

put you in touch with a salon that offers apprenticeships.

Job Placement Services

If apprenticing doesn't sound right for you, make an appointment with your school's director to talk about *job placement*. Most schools provide a placement service for their students. Your director or career counselor will be able to tell you which salons are looking to hire new personnel. He or she will also help you choose a salon that's right for you and your particular talents. Schools are often contacted by area salons and asked to recommend a student for a position.

The Classifieds

In addition to using your school's service, look in the *classified section* of area newspapers for job listings. Call salons and inquire about any future openings. Ask to speak to the salon's manager and be polite and pleasant.

Interviews

Once an *interview* has been scheduled, be sure to get a good night's rest the night before. You want to look and feel good about yourself during your interview. Think about all the positive qualities and talents that you possess.

During the interview, demonstrate your warm personality and an eagerness to learn and grow. Dress and behave professionally. Some salon owners like to observe you cut and style hair. A demonstration like this is usually set up after an initial interview, and you might be asked to get your own models. Give some thought to this ahead of time so that you're prepared.

Have confidence in yourself and your training. You have studied and trained for hundreds of hours to get where you are. You've practiced long and hard and are equipped with a solid foundation and understanding of cosmetology. Your state has given you permission to practice cosmetology because you have passed a rigorous state licensing exam. Take pride in what you've already accomplished as you take the next step. You're ready!

Questions to Ask Yourself

There are different ways to go about getting a job in your chosen field. 1) What are they? 2) How can the school or program that you trained with help you get a job? 3) What is an apprenticeship? 4) Do any of the salons in your community offer apprenticeships?

Glossary

apprentice   Person learning a skill or trade from an expert by working for the expert for a certain length of time.

aromatherapy   Beauty treatments that are made from pleasant fragrances.

commission   Percentage of money taken in on sales that is kept by the cosmetologist.

consultant   Person who gives technical or professional advice.

cosmetology   Study of hair, skin, nails, and products related to their care.

dandruff   Dry skin on a person's scalp.

esthetician   Expert or specialist in beauty.

freelance   Independent worker who is not under contract with any one employer.

franchise   Chain of salons that have the same name and style of service.

mentor   Professional who acts as teacher to a person new to a field.

résumé   Summary of one's education, training, and work experience.

scholarship   Gift of money to help a student continue his or her studies.

For More Information

Cosmetology Advancement Foundation
208 E. 51st Street
New York, NY 10022

National Beauty Career Center
3839 White Plains Road
Bronx, NY 19467
(718) 330-1280

National Hairdressers and Cosmetologists
    Association
3510 Live Street
St. Louis, MO 63103
(314) 534-1170

For Further Reading

Fornay, Alfred. *Guide to Skin Care and Makeup for Women of Color*. New York: Simon and Schuster, 1989.

Harper, Victoria. *Professional by Choice: Milady's Career Development Guide*. Albany, NY: Milady Publishing Co., 1994.

Johnson, Barbara L. *Careers in Beauty Culture*. New York: Rosen Publishing Group, 1989.

Murphy-Martin, Mary. *Planning Your Cosmetology Career*. Englewood Cliffs, NJ: Prentice-Hall Careers and Technology, 1994.

Rudman, Jack. *Rudman's Questions and Answers on the Occupational Competency Exam in Cosmetology*. New York: National Learning Corporation, 1992.

Index

Acknowledgments
I'd like to extend heartfelt thanks to the devoted owners and staff of the Scott Miller Salon in Rochester, New York. Their generosity of time and talent is greatly appreciated. Many thanks to Kathy Didas of the Continental School of Beauty Culture and JoAnne Ryan and Nancy Leiter of the Eastern Monroe Career Center for their expertise and time.

About the Author
Jeanne M. Strazzabosco is a freelance writer and translator.
    Ms. Strazzabosco has written three books for young adults. She is a French and Spanish teacher in Rochester, New York, where she lives with her husband and family.

Photo Credits: Cover, p. 28 © Bill Stanton/International Stock; p. 2 © Martha Tabor/Impact Visuals; pp. 6, 16, 45, 55 © AP/Wide World Photos; p. 11 © White/Pite/International Stock; pp. 19, 23, 25 © Wayne Sproul/International Stock; pp. 31, 38, 52 © Wilson North/International Stock; pp. 40, 57 © George Ancona/International Stock.

Design: Erin McKenna

WGRL-HQ JUV
31057904028530
J 331.7 STRAZ
Strazzabosco, Jeanne.
Choosing a career in
cosmetology
J 640.

Strazzabosco, Jeanne.
    WEST GEORGIA REGIONAL LIBRARY